Welcome message

It is with great pleasure that I introduce you to this beautifully illustrated biographical book about the life and times of our honorable and respected leader, His Highness Sheikh Khalifa bin Zayed Al Nahyan, President of the United Arab Emirates and Ruler of Abu Dhabi.

This book is the first-of-its-kind and contains rare photographs and insights into the brilliant life of a true visionary leader, a leader who not only fosters a culture of progress and development while remaining true to the traditional Arabian values of hospitality and respecting other nations and religions, but a leader who guides the nation with a generous heart and a scholarly mind.

Under his wise direction, Abu Dhabi has taken its place on the world stage as a desirable destination for investment, commerce and tourism. Since His Highness graciously assumed the most honorable positions bestowed upon him, interest in the prosperous Emirate of Abu Dhabi and the exciting and diverse portfolio of projects, both locally and internationally, continues to grow.

This includes the range of developments underway at Abu Dhabi Airports Company (ADAC), which is responsible for the operations of the UAE's capital gateway, Abu Dhabi International Airport, Al Ain International Airport, Al Bateen Executive Airport and Sir Bani Yas and Delma Island Airports located on the Desert Islands in Al Gharbia region.

Currently, a large scale AED 25 billion (USD 6.8 billion) re-development and expansion plan underway at Abu Dhabi International Airport has been designed to increase the overall capacity of the airport in line with predicted demand, to more than 20 million passengers per year.

This book offers an exceptional opportunity to delve deeper into the esteemed life of our beloved visionary, H.H. Sheikh Khalifa bin Zayed Al Nahyan, and Abu Dhabi Airports Company is honoured to provide our support for this publication.

Khalifa Al Mazrouei
Chairman
Abu Dhabi Airports Company (ADAC)

SHEIKH KHALIFA

LIFE AND TIMES

With compliments of

شركة أبوظبي للمطارات
ABU DHABI AIRPORTS COMPANY

SHEIKH KHALIFA

LIFE AND TIMES

BY ROYAL PHOTOGRAPHER
NOOR ALI RASHID

MOTIVATE
PUBLISHING

Published by Motivate Publishing

Dubai: PO Box 2331, Dubai, UAE
Tel: (+971 4) 282 4060, fax: (+971 4) 282 0428
E-mail: books@motivate.ae www.booksarabia.com

Office 508, Building No 8, Dubai Media City, Dubai, UAE
Tel: (+971 4) 390 3550, fax: (+971 4) 390 4845

Abu Dhabi: PO Box 43072, Abu Dhabi, UAE
Tel: (+971 2) 677 2005, fax: (+971 2) 677 0124

London: Acre House, 11/15 William Road, London NW1 3ER
E-mail: motivateuk@motivate.ae

Directors: Obaid Humaid Al Tayer and Ian Fairservice

Researched and written by Pippa Sanderson
Editorial Adviser: Peter Hellyer

Consultant Editor: David Steele
Deputy Editor: Moushumi Nandy
Assistant Editor: Zelda Pinto
Art Director: Andrea Willmore
Senior Designer: Cithadel Francisco

General Manager Books: Jonathan Griffiths

Author's Team
Photo Archivist: Shamsa Rashid
Photo Researcher: Samia Rashid
Editorial Coordinator: Yasmin Rashid

© Noor Ali Rashid and Motivate Publishing 2007
First Published 2007
Reprinted 2007, 2008

Originally published with the support and encouragement of Mubadala
Investment Company.

ISBN: 978 1 86063 200 6

British Library Cataloguing-in-Publication Data.
A catalogue record for this book is available from the British Library.

Printed and bound in the UAE by Emirates Printing Press, Dubai.

Dedication

*This book is respectfully dedicated to HH Sheikh Khalifa bin
Zayed Al Nahyan, President of the United Arab Emirates
and Ruler of Abu Dhabi, and the Al Nahyan family, with
sincere gratitude for their support over half a century.*

Noor Ali Rashid

Other Motivate titles by Noor Ali Rashid

Abu Dhabi – Life & Times
Dubai – Life & Times
The UAE – Visions of Change
Sheikh Zayed – Life and Times
Sheikh Maktoum – Life and Times

This spread: *Qasr al-Hosn, the ancestral home of the Al Nahyan
ruling family in Abu Dhabi.*

Contents

HH Sheikh Mohammed bin Rashid Al Maktoum

Sheikh Khalifa . . .
the leader and the man

A tribute from HH Sheikh Mohammed bin Rashid Al Maktoum

No matter how much I say about my brother, His Highness Sheikh Khalifa bin Zayed Al Nahyan – may God grant him long life – my testimony will always be inadequate. Nevertheless, the accomplishments of His Highness are well known to all and speak clearly for themselves.

He is the leader who has succeeded with his competence and ability in filling the huge void left by the departure of Sheikh Zayed bin Sultan Al Nahyan. In achieving this Sheikh Khalifa has demonstrated he is a most worthy successor to a great predecessor.

He is the statesman whose enlightened vision has allowed the United Arab Emirates to continue to progress and prosper during a period of rapid and fundamental change in the world.

He is the leader who takes every opportunity to support the causes of the Arab and Islamic nations.

He is the father who spares no effort to secure prosperity for his country.

Above all else, he is the man who works tirelessly for the interests and welfare of his people.

The influence of Sheikh Khalifa and his enlightened vision were evident many years before he assumed the leadership of the UAE on the second of November 2004. They began early in the reign of the late Sheikh Zayed. Since the founding of the UAE, Sheikh Khalifa has played a pivotal role in formulating and directing the various policies and strategies that have earned the UAE respect among the global community.

Under the wise leadership of Sheikh Khalifa, the United Arab Emirates continues to move forward on the same path established by the late Sheikh Zayed.

This is the path that has led to the UAE's pioneering development policies, to its positive role in promoting regional cooperation, and to its balanced policies and position on the international stage.

The UAE has become an international centre of growing importance in finance, business, commerce, tourism and service. The country has also developed an outstanding system of social welfare and has become an oasis of security and stability, as well as an example of successful development and progress. Internationally the UAE has steadfastly supported and advanced Arab and Islamic causes.

We are fully confident in our ability to achieve the ambitious goals of our people under the leadership of His Highness Sheikh Khalifa bin Zayed Al Nahayan.

Mohammed bin Rashid Al Maktoum
Vice-President and Prime Minister of the UAE
Ruler of Dubai

HH Sheikh Mohammed bin Zayed Al Nahyan

Preface

It is with great pleasure that I introduce this book about my brother, my President and my leader – a man who embodies the hopes and aspirations of the people of the United Arab Emirates. The President, His Highness Sheikh Khalifa bin Zayed Al Nahyan, is one of the principal leaders in the modern history of the UAE. He is a man of great vision. He is, in addition, a man of action, of intellect, bravery and compassion. We are extremely proud he is our President and we are fortunate to have the benefit of his guidance, wisdom and leadership.

We were blessed to have our late father, Sheikh Zayed bin Sultan Al Nahyan as the founding President of the UAE. Sheikh Zayed, may Allah grant him His blessings, was a great leader. His vision and concern for the welfare of his people led to the effective use of our natural resources to serve the interests of the nation's citizens. Under Sheikh Zayed's historic leadership, our country moved forward faster, in terms of economic development, than any other country in the history of the world. We are again blessed that, following Sheikh Zayed's departure, the leadership of our country passed on to Sheikh Khalifa, who shares the values of our late father and continues his bold vision for our country.

His Highness Sheikh Khalifa was the Crown Prince of Abu Dhabi when the UAE was founded in 1971. In that role, and now as President, he has had a major impact on the country during the last four decades. He led in the building of the UAE as a place that welcomes people from all round the world, a place of harmony and safety, and a land where we see gleaming cities and lush greenery where once there was only desert. Sheikh Khalifa led in the creation of the physical infrastructure that provides our citizens with modern roads, schools, hospitals, airports and telecommunications. Equally important, he led in the creation of our social infrastructure that values human develop-

ment, knowledge, peace and global understanding.

Sheikh Khalifa is leading our country at a time of extraordinary change in our region and the world. He understands the challenges our country faces, and is able to lead us in understanding those challenges and in fashioning responses that serve our country well. The wise, strong leadership of Sheikh Khalifa has been instrumental in making Abu Dhabi and the UAE a place of progress, prosperity and stability. Under his leadership, our country has become a positive force for regional and global cooperation, and for the peaceful resolution of conflicts round the world.

Sheikh Khalifa – Life and Times is well presented and enjoyable to read. Noor Ali Rashid combines his legendary photographic talents with a beautifully written text. Many of the images in this book will cause us to swell with honour and pride. I am confident *Sheikh Khalifa – Life and Times* will be welcomed by readers everywhere. It tells the story of a man of our times who I am proud to call my brother and my President.

Mohammed bin Zayed Al Nahyan
Crown Prince of Abu Dhabi
Deputy Supreme Commander of the Armed Forces

The development of Abu Dhabi

Drilling for water on the edge of the Empty Quarter.

The largest and wealthiest of the seven emirates that make up the United Arab Emirates, Abu Dhabi has a rich, eventful history. Excavations by the Abu Dhabi Island Archaeological Survey (ADIAS), the Al Ain Department of Antiquities and Tourism and foreign teams have identified sites that date back to the Late Stone Age and beyond, indicating the inhabitants of this area have, for at least 5,000 years, depended on the resources of the sea, the resources of the desert and its oases, and trading, to make a living.

Skilled divers began to harvest the fine pearls of the Arabian Gulf at least as early as 4000 BC. In addition, the ingenious invention of irrigation channels – *aflaj* – permitted agriculture to continue in Abu Dhabi's inland oasis of Al Ain even after the environment began to become more arid at around 5000 BC.

Groups of people had migrated into the area from Yemen and central Arabia by the second century AD, adapting their own traditions to the environment and surroundings they found. Although the discovery by ADIAS of a pre-Islamic Nestorian monastery on the island of Sir Bani Yas shows that at least some of these migrants became Christian, the arrival of Islam in the middle of the 7th-century AD brought a new faith to the people, one which they eventually adopted. It has remained a solid cornerstone of their beliefs – and their way of life – ever since.

The Bani Yas

The first trace of the Emirate of Abu Dhabi in history dates back to the 16th-century AD, when a book by a travelling court jeweller from Venice mentioned a list of islands in the southern Arabian Gulf. To one of them he gave the name Sirbeniast – or Sir Bani Yas – evidence that the Bani Yas confederation of tribes, led for the last 250 years by the family of the President of the UAE, His Highness Sheikh Khalifa bin Zayed Al Nahyan, had achieved a degree of prominence in the region.

The Bani Yas themselves first appeared in history in the early 17th century, when they are reported to have been involved in a major battle, between the coast and inland Liwa Oases, with an advancing army from Oman in 1633. Historical records trace the origins of the Al Nahyan (part of the Al Bu Falah, a small subsection of the Bani Yas tribe), rulers of what was to become the Emirate of Abu Dhabi at least as far back as the late 17th or early 18th century, to the reign of a somewhat mysterious figure named Nahyan, the paramount sheikh. He was succeeded by a son, Isa and, by the middle of the 18th century, his son, Dhiyab bin Isa, had become the sheikh of the Bani Yas, with his main base in the Liwa Oases, deep in the desert.

The founding of Abu Dhabi

To Sheikh Dhiyab goes the credit of establishing the location for the present-day island city of Abu Dhabi, believed to have been founded in 1761. A tribal legend tells the tale of a party of hunters from the Liwa Oases who visited the coast and saw the tracks of a gazelle leading out across the *sabkha* (salt flats). The tracks led to a narrow inlet of the sea, which they crossed, to an island just offshore. Their pursuit continued and, following the tracks through a thick sea mist, they came upon the gazelle drinking at a spring.

While the tale does not relate what happened to the gazelle, the discovery of water on an offshore island was far more significant. Returning to Liwa, the hunters reported their find to Sheikh Dhiyab. Recognizing its significance, he ordered a settlement be established on the island, which he named Abu Dhabi, meaning either 'Possession of the Gazelle' (*dhabi* means gazelle in Arabic), 'Home of the Gazelle', or 'Father of the Gazelle'.

The choice was fortunate. The Bani Yas and their allies, the Manasir, already controlled the Liwa Oases as well as some western islands such as Dalma and Sir Bani Yas. Between Dalma and Abu Dhabi lay some of the greatest oyster beds in the whole of the southern Gulf and, with an Abu Dhabi base, Sheikh Dhiyab and his successors were able to benefit from the revenues of the pearling industry. To consolidate his position, Sheikh Dhiyab's son, Sheikh Shakhbut, moved his headquarters to Abu Dhabi in 1795, building a small fort that survives to this day, much enlarged, as Qasr al-Hosn. Built to enclose the original freshwater source, the fort remained the Al Nahyan's seat of power, and home, until as recently as 1966.

The advent of the British

Offshore, following the arrival of the British on the scene at the beginning of the 19th century, the frequent scuffles on the pearling banks, which had interrupted the emirate's main source of income, were brought to a halt with the ratification of a Perpetual Treaty of Maritime Truce in 1853.

From that treaty the area became known as the Trucial Coast or the Trucial States, a name that survived until the

formation of the United Arab Emirates in 1971.

By the end of the 19th century, the island town of Abu Dhabi had more pearling boats than anywhere else on the coast. Ruled between 1855 and 1909 by Sheikh Zayed bin Khalifa – Zayed the Great – the grandson of Sheikh Shakhbut bin Dhiyab, the emirate was a centre of power and, by the standards of the time, of wealth.

Inland, the Al Nahyan sheikhs extended their influence to the oasis of Al Ain, where they formed an alliance with the Dhawahir tribe and acquired property.

The nine oases of the Al Ain/Buraimi area are spread over a considerable area in the north-east corner of the Arabian Peninsula. The actual village of Buraimi, lends its name to the surrounding territory and the village, along with two others, belongs to the Sultanate of Oman, with the rest of the area belonging to the Al Nahyan family of Abu Dhabi. A focal point for major tribes, possession of the oases, with their priceless water sources, accompanying date-palm and other plantations (and, in the early 1950s, the possible existence of oil), were strategically important and vital for survival. Consequently, ownership of the land had been the cause of several tribal skirmishes in the past.

However, when Sheikh Zayed bin Khalifa passed away on May 19, 1909, Abu Dhabi's fortunes took a turn for the worse with political instability, tribal feuds and fratricide, and the next four rulers, all brothers – Tahnoon bin Zayed (1909–1912), Hamdan bin Zayed (1912–1922), Sultan bin Zayed (1922–1926) and Saqr bin Zayed (1926–1928) – followed Zayed the Great in quick succession.

Stability returns

Sheikh Shakhbut bin Sultan took over the reins from his uncle in 1928. In his early 20s at the time, he was the eldest of four sons, of which Sheikh Zayed (the father of Sheikh Khalifa, the current President of the UAE and Ruler of Abu Dhabi) was the youngest. To cement his rule, the brothers took an oath at the behest of their mother – Sheikha Salamah bint Butti – to support and defend the new sheikh and never again to resort to violence to resolve family quarrels. This pledge restored stability to the sheikhdom.

In 1929, Sheikh Shakhbut allowed the British Royal Air Force (RAF) access to his sheltered coastal waters and the RAF used them to land several flying boats. These were joined by other military aircraft after the RAF had established a strategic landing strip and refuelling facilities on Sir Bani Yas Island. Several years later, the RAF established another base on a long stretch of *sabkha* to the south of Abu Dhabi.

The 1930s were a bleak decade for the region: the world depression affected the level of Middle East trade, and the introduction of the cultured pearl from Japan suffocated the local pearl-diving industry which, at one point, accounted for some 95 per cent of Abu Dhabi's total income. As a result, the 15,000 or so souls living in the town were plunged into abject poverty; many of whom became ill or even died.

When the first oil-company teams arrived from Great Britain to carry out preliminary surveys, their timing couldn't have been better and Sheikh Zayed was assigned by Sheikh Shakhbut to guide them through the desert – giving him his first exposure to the industry that was to have such a profound effect on the country in years to come.

The fight for oil

In 1939, on the eve of the Second World War, Sheikh Shakhbut, realizing the financial potential, granted the first oil concession for his territory. Yet, with no properly defined borders between the sheikhdoms (there had never been a need for any until now), disagreements between the ruling sheikhs were inevitable. Sheikh Shakhbut maintained his territory stretched as far north-east as Jebel Ali, while the Ruler of Dubai, Sheikh Saeed bin Maktoum, believed his sheikhdom extended some 40 kilometres south-west of Jebel Ali to Khaur Ghanadhah. Although both rulers were keen to resolve their differences cordially, the discord caused great tension.

The onset of the Second World War on September 3, 1939 meant the postponement of fledgling oil-prospecting operations which had provided the sheikhdom with a lifeline and much-needed revenue and, for the greater part, a suspension of the border dispute between Abu Dhabi and Dubai. Although they were not directly involved during the Second World War, the strategic location of the sheikhdoms and the possibility of oil meant more and more allied troops arrived in the area, particularly troops from Britain, which feared German interference in Iraq and Iran and perceived a threat to its Indian trade routes.

When the war ended in 1945, the task of re-establishing oil-field operations began for the British. In 1946, Sheikh Shakhbut appointed his brother, Sheikh Zayed, to the position of Ruler's Representative in Abu Dhabi's Eastern Region, based in Al Ain.

In 1950, onshore drilling commenced at Ra's Sadr on the north-east coast of Abu Dhabi but this proved to be a dry hole, as was a second hole at Shuweihat near Jebel Dhanna. Meanwhile, Sheikh Shakhbut awarded Abu Dhabi's first offshore oil concession in 1951.

The possibility of the discovery of oil brought with it territorial disputes and, in 1955, Saudi Arabia renewed its claim to the Buraimi Oases near Al Ain, belonging to Muscat and Oman (as it was then known). The British supported Abu Dhabi and Muscat and Oman in asserting their sovereignty, and the Buraimi Dispute, as it became known, saw British military force being used alongside the local forces to expel the Saudis.

Prospecting for oil continued and, in 1957, British Petroleum's (BP) mobile drilling platform, the *Adma* (Abu Dhabi Marine Areas) *Enterprise*, measuring 61 metres in length and 30 metres in width, and designed to operate in some 24 metres of water, was towed from The Netherlands, through the Suez Canal and into the Arabian Gulf. Arriving at Das Island, located 140 km offshore from Abu Dhabi, it underwent its final fit out and, from there, it was moved into position in the offshore Umm Shaif field, in January 1958, to begin drilling.

The field bore oil less than three months later, bringing with it the promise of extraordinary wealth. In 1960, oil was also discovered onshore at a well on the Murban structure west of Abu Dhabi island, proving the commercial viability of what was to become known as the Bab field. The first cargo of crude oil was exported from Abu Dhabi in 1962 and, from then on, oil has dominated the economy. Today, Abu Dhabi produces more than 90 per cent of the country's oil and it is estimated it has supplies for another 150 years.

Cautious, with a frugal style, the conservative Sheikh Shakhbut was ill-equipped to adapt to the changes this discovery brought about and the Al Nahyan family decided it was time for him to make way for a new leader. There was only one man for the job – Sheikh Shakhbut's brother and Sheikh Khalifa's father, Sheikh Zayed bin Sultan – who was inaugurated as Ruler of Abu Dhabi on August 6, 1966.

In November 1967, Abu Dhabi joined OPEC (the Organisation of Petroleum Exporting Countries), which was established in September 1960.

The British withdraw

Early in 1968, the British Government, under the leadership of the Labour Party's Harold Wilson, gave notice that Britain would withdraw its forces from the area east of Suez by the end of 1971. This was done in order to reduce defence expenditure, which had been criticized by others in the party. The ruling sheikhs of the Trucial States, Bahrain and Qatar were stunned and set about trying to decide the best course of action to take after the British left. The idea of a federation between the Gulf States was mooted.

This was taken forward by Sheikh Zayed bin Sultan Al Nahyan, the Ruler of Abu Dhabi, and Sheikh Rashid bin

Saeed Al Maktoum, the Ruler of Dubai, who met for talks on February 18, 1968, at the border of the two sheikhdoms. The two rulers invited the rulers from neighbouring sheikhdoms in Sharjah, Fujairah, Ra's al-Khaimah, Ajman and Umm al-Qaiwain, along with Bahrain and Qatar, to join them in creating a larger federation. One week later the nine rulers met in Dubai for two days, keen to cooperate with one another, put aside past differences and seek strength through unity.

At the end of the meeting on February 27, 1968, all nine rulers signed an agreement that would set in motion the creation of a federation. Between May 18 and 19, another meeting was convened in Abu Dhabi between the rulers' advisers, where they established that, although each state's differences were significant, everyone was in favour of creating a federation.

Further meetings and committees were called during the next couple of years to iron-out differences and to garner accord for constitutional issues and compromise, which would see the birth of a federation before the British left for good. On October 24, 1970, the deputy rulers of the nine states gathered in Abu Dhabi for a meeting to discuss several contentious issues, including Union Council representation and the location of the new capital (it was proposed to construct the new capital at the border between Abu Dhabi and Dubai). The meeting was hosted by the 22-year-old Sheikh Khalifa bin Zayed Al Nahyan.

However, at the end of 1970, the prospect that nine states could create a workable federation was looking somewhat shaky. By mid-June 1971, Bahrain informed its prospective partners that it would go it alone, declaring independence on August 14, 1971, followed by Qatar on September 1, 1971.

Meanwhile, on July 10, 1971, the rulers of the seven Trucial States met in Dubai to formalize the transfer of several government functions, including exchange controls, the licensing of alcohol for its consumption by non-Muslims, police coordination and, crucially, federation. At the end of the meeting, the Ruler of Ra's al-Khaimah, Sheikh Saqr bin Mohammed, declined to sign the provisional constitution, unlike the other six rulers who all put pen to paper.

The birth of a nation

On December 1, the treaties between Britain and the seven Trucial States came to an end (although they were replaced by a new agreement with the UAE) and, on December 2, 1971, the rulers of the six emirates from Abu Dhabi, Ajman, Dubai, Fujairah, Sharjah and Umm al-Qaiwain announced the formation of the new state, the United Arab Emirates (UAE), and named Abu Dhabi's Sheikh Zayed bin Sultan Al

Nahyan as its first President, with Dubai's Sheikh Rashid bin Saeed Al Maktoum the new country's Vice-President. Negotiations continued with Ra's al-Khaimah and the sheikhdom became the seventh emirate to join the UAE on February 10, 1972. Four days after the birth of the new nation, the UAE became a member of the Arab League and, on December 9, it joined the United Nations.

In the presence of rulers and citizens, the national flag of the United Arab Emirates is raised for the first time in the morning of December 2, 1971. The building in the background is known as Union House.

ABOVE: Modern Al Ain taking shape in the 1960s, together with some of its main arteries.

PREVIOUS SPREAD: Returning home with the groceries. This fort, Husn Sultan, with its square enclosures and round corner towers, is a fine example of a type common in the Al Ain region.

There was always plenty for the young sheikh to do and paperwork was never far away.
Here we see Sheikh Khalifa bin Zayed Al Nahyan in his office in Al Ain.

ABOVE: Al Ain in the late 1960s. While working as Ruler's Representative in the Eastern Region, Sheikh Zayed ordered the planting of a great number of trees as part of a visionary town plan. This early picture shows the progress of the project, which has since resulted in Al Ain being one of the greenest and most pleasant cities in Arabia.

OPPOSITE PAGE, TOP LEFT: The stance of the sentry looks considerably more permanent and solid than the crumbling fortress, made from stone, straw and mud, in the background.

OPPOSITE PAGE, TOP RIGHT: Sheikh Zayed's palace in Al Ain.

OPPOSITE PAGE, BOTTOM : Bedouin from the Omani town of Buraimi visiting the Al Ain market.

Aʙᴏᴠᴇ: Camel races at Al Ain. Jostling camel jockeys make a frenzied spurt along the final furlong to the finish. The sport remains popular today.

Tᴏᴘ ʟᴇғᴛ: Bedouin and their mounts – camels were essential to the survival of man in the Arabian desert and well looked after by their owners.

Tᴏᴘ ʀɪɢʜᴛ: Al Ain's camel market is still one of the largest in the country.

In his position as Ruler's Representative in the Eastern Region, Sheikh Zayed bin Sultan initiated the construction and renovation of a*flaj*, such as Falaj al-Dawoodi in Al Ain, seen in this photograph. The local people were quick to use these irrigation channels for bathing and watering their livestock.

Top left: Drilling for water in Abu Dhabi.

Top right: Pumped water is used for farms, gardens and for domestic purposes.

Bottom left: Al Ain is justifiably known as the 'Oasis City', and boasts plenty of water and lush farms in its surrounding areas.

Bottom right: A field irrigated by a *falaj* on the outskirts of Al Ain.

Opposite page, top: The construction of roads and buildings in Al Ain began soon after the discovery of oil, transforming it into a lively town.

Opposite page, bottom: An ornamental garden takes shape in Al Ain.

Hard bargaining has always been a prerequisite for shopping in the souks of Al Ain.

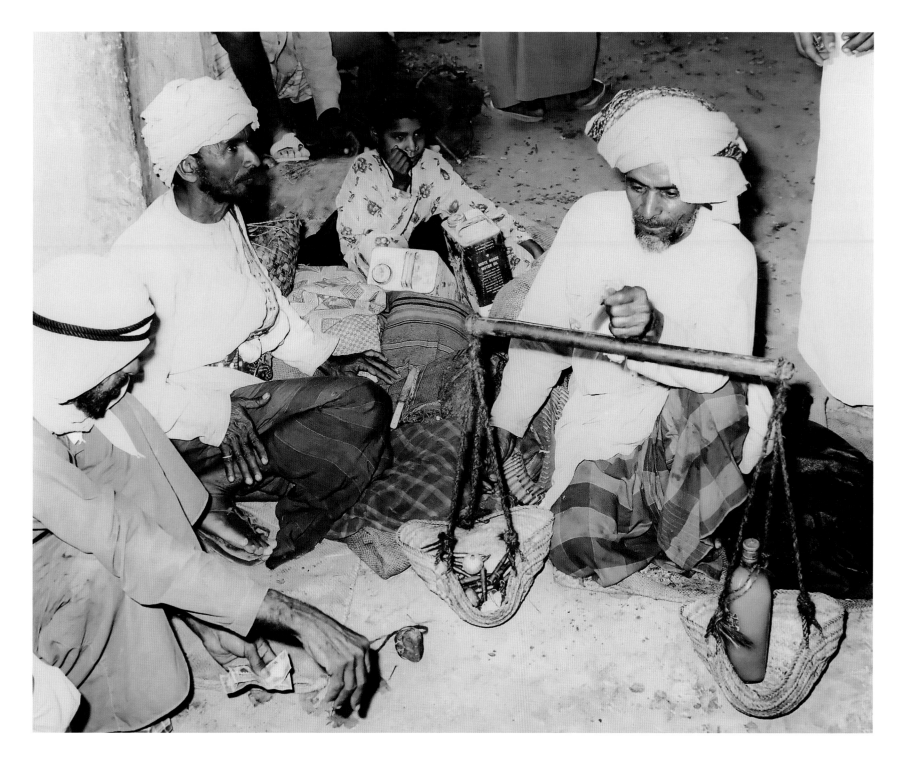

Fair dealing in the souk – bullets and bottled ghee balance the scales.

Pottery similar to these jugs has been made in Al Ain for at least 5,000 years.

To maintain the security of the area, the inhabitants constructed several forts, including Fort Al Jahili pictured here. Most were built of mud brick on a stone base to which the builders added decorative patterns, arches, crenellated walls and latticework screens.

A confident, young Sheikh Khalifa welcomes a visiting VIP to his Al Ain *majlis*. Seen in the centre is Dr Saif Al Wadi, Deputy Director of the Amiri Court.

Sheikh Khalifa watching army manoeuvres at Al Ain with the Chief of Staff, Abu Dhabi Defence Force, Sheikh Faisal bin Sultan Al Qasimi.

ABOVE: Brothers Sheikh Khalifa and Sheikh Mohammed bin Zayed Al Nahyan on official duty during a military graduation ceremony in Al Ain.

LEFT: Graduates from the Sheikh Zayed Military Academy in Al Ain pose for a picture with Sheikh Khalifa bin Zayed Al Nahyan, centre; Sheikh Mohammed bin Rashid Al Maktoum, to his right; Sheikh Mohammed bin Zayed Al Nahyan, to the right of Sheikh Mohammed bin Rashid Al Maktoum; Sheikh Sultan bin Zayed Al Nahyan, to Sheikh Khalifa's left; and Sheikh Tahnoun bin Mohammed Al Nahyan, to Sheikh Sultan's left.

Camels were once an essential ally in the struggle to survive in the desert, providing transport, milk, meat, wool, leather and even dung for fuel. They were also used in battle and for sport. No wonder they are still held in such high regard today.

ABOVE: These two tribesmen sport the essential accessories – ornate *khanjars* (curved daggers), rifles and well-stocked bandoleers.

RIGHT: Members of the Abu Dhabi Defence Force stand guard at Al Maqta'a Checkpoint, on the mainland. Abu Dhabi Island was previously connected to the mainland by the Al Maqta'a Causeway, but the old causeway has now been replaced by a pair of bridges which carry heavy volumes of traffic each day.

LEFT: During his first days as Ruler in 1966, people wait patiently to greet Sheikh Zayed at the gates of Qasr al-Hosn.

OPPOSITE PAGE: Qasr al-Hosn, the imposing fortress and ancestral home of the ruling Al Nahyan family in Abu Dhabi, shown here decorated on the occasion of Sheikh Zayed's Accession on August 6, 1966.

ABOVE: The settlements in Abu Dhabi slowly changed from 'arish (barasti) huts and coral houses, to modern buildings and then towering skyscapers.

OPPOSITE PAGE, TOP: A camel caravan bringing produce from the interior to the souk.

OPPOSITE PAGE, BOTTOM: Construction work starting on the Abu Dhabi Corniche in 1967.

Top left: Das Island's airstrip, some 140 km from the mainland. It was the search for oil which gave the modern aviation industry in the Gulf its foundations.

Top right: Oil pipelines being laid as part of the transformation of Das Island.

Above left: All equipment had to be brought to the island by air or sea from Bahrain.

Above right: An aerial view of the accomodation on Das Island in the late 1960s. Prior to the discovery of oil, Das was a remote, uninhabited, rocky island with no fresh water. Its landscape changed forever once it was chosen as the supply base for the Umm Shaif oilfield and the harbour, airstrip, supply base, housing and hospital were all constructed.

Opposite page: Crude oil was piped from Umm Shaif field to Das for loading on the tankers.

LEFT AND TOP: Abu Dhabi in transition. When these photographs were taken in 1969 the shape that the modern city was to take was already visible. The Corniche had recently been completed and most of the other main roads were already in place.

ABOVE: Apart from the familiar shape of Qasr al-Hosn, it is hard to reconcile the Abu Dhabi of yesteryear with today's sophisticated city.

The foundations of the Al Maqta'a Bridge under construction. The old watchtower that guarded the approach to Abu Dhabi island can be seen in the background.

The main span of Al Maqta'a Bridge begins to take shape. In the background is the mainland Customs House which still remains standing today.

ABOVE: Accompanied by officials, Sheikh Zayed takes King Hussein of Jordan on a tour of Al Maqta'a Bridge during its final stages of construction.

OPPOSITE PAGE, TOP: A guard of honour awaiting an official dignitary at the Bateen Airport.

OPPOSITE PAGE, BOTTOM: Sheikh Zayed's Royal Guards at Qasr al-Hosn palace, Abu Dhabi in 1966.

Sheikh Hamdan bin Mohammed bin Khalifa Al Nahyan with his children. During Sheikh Zayed's rule, he held important portfolios in the government, including municipality, education and health. He was Deputy Prime Minister in Sheikh Rashid's first government.

Sheikh Mubarak bin Mohammed Al Nahyan, right, and Sheikh Hamdan bin Mohammed Al Nahyan, centre, at the Abu Dhabi Airport. Abdul Jalil Al Fahim is on the extreme left. Sheikh Mubarak was formerly the Police Commander and the UAE's first MInister of the Interior.

The new Abu Dhabi Airport, situated near the Al Maqta'a Bridge, was opened in 1969.
Replacing a sand strip near today's National Theatre and TV station, it served the capital
until 1982, when an even newer airport was opened on the mainland.

Partly visible under construction, in the foreground in 1974, is the Sheikh Khalifa Mosque, while the Mohammed bin Zayed Building – later to be dwarfed by the Baynunah Tower and Arab Monetary Fund Building – rises beyond the British Embassy compound.

TOP LEFT: **Abu Dhabi in the late 1960s. With the laying out of roads, more vehicles came into use.**

TOP RIGHT: **A nation in transition – the old and new meet in front of the Eastern Bank.**

ABOVE LEFT AND RIGHT: **Development of Al Salam Street in Abu Dhabi in the late 1960s.**

OPPOSITE PAGE, TOP LEFT AND RIGHT: **The Abu Dhabi Corniche in the mid 1960s before construction (left) and upon initial completion (right).**

OPPOSITE PAGE, CENTRE LEFT: **The Abu Dhabi Coast Guard carries out routine coastal checks.**

OPPOSITE PAGE, CENTRE RIGHT: **The Customs House on Abu Dhabi's Corniche.**

OPPOSITE PAGE, BOTTOM LEFT: **Qasr al-Hosn in the 1960s. The fort was originally constructed in 1795.**

OPPOSITE PAGE, BOTTOM RIGHT: **Sheikh Hamdan Street decorated for Sheikh Zayed's Accession Day.**

A guard at Jashanmal store, one of the oldest surviving stores in the emirate and, in this photo, decorated with lights and flags on the occasion of Sheikh Zayed's Accession Day.

Jama Mosque, Abu Dhabi's main mosque, with the historic Qasr al-Hosn in the background.
The city currently boasts more than 400 mosques, with others under construction.

ABOVE: Abu Dhabi Corniche after its initial construction. By 2006 it had been completely rebuilt.

OPPOSITE PAGE, TOP: A presidential motorcade leaving Al Musharaf Palace in Abu Dhabi.

OPPOSITE PAGE, BOTTOM: Dancers celebrate Sheikh Mohammed bin Zayed Al Nahyan's wedding.

Above: Whether rowing or under sail, traditional boat races regularly draw a keen crowd of spectators as the people of Abu Dhabi have always had strong links with the sea.

Opposite page: A victory lap at the UIM Abu Dhabi World F-1 Power Boat Grand Prix 1993.

ABOVE: The state-of-the-art Emirates Palace hotel is Abu Dhabi's first 'seven star' hotel.

OPPOSITE PAGE, TOP: Abu Dhabi continues to grow and evolve, a city of parks and high-rise buildings juxtaposed with elegant mosques.

OPPOSITE PAGE, BOTTOM: A number of new buildings that encompass contemporary design and facilities have been constructed along the Corniche and breakwaters of the city of Abu Dhabi.

Close to Al Maqta'a Bridge, the magnificent Sheikh Zayed Grand Mosque is one of the world's largest mosques and features Makran marble facades. When finished, this new Abu Dhabi landmark will be able to accommodate some 40,000 worshippers.

The view of Abu Dhabi's tall buildings give a whole new perspective to the city, and the incredible development of this desert island can be appreciated in full. It is very easy to forget that this was once a flat, barren stretch of sand.

The grooming of a President

Sheikh Khalifa leaving Qasr al-Hosn after meeting his uncle and former Ruler of Abu Dhabi, Sheikh Shakhbut bin Sultan Al Nahyan.

Sheikh Khalifa (meaning approximately 'to render stewardship' or 'protect the same things as God') bin Zayed Al Nahyan, President of the UAE and Ruler of Abu Dhabi, was born in 1948 in Al Ain in Abu Dhabi's Eastern Province, and is the eldest son of Sheikh Zayed bin Sultan Al Nahyan and the only son of Sheikha Hassa bint Mohammed bin Khalifa Al Nahyan.

Located inland some 160 kilometres from Abu Dhabi, Al Ain (Arabic for 'The Spring'), with its numerous oases, has been a focal point for wandering Bedouin for centuries, and its origins have been dated back some 7,000 years with the discovery of numerous sites of archaeological importance. Today, Al Ain is the largest conurbation, or extended urban area, in the emirate's Eastern Province and is known as 'The Oasis City'. The city is also home to the UAE University and boasts the country's largest museum and zoo, not to mention some wonderful old buildings and forts.

Life in Al Ain and other settlements, before the discovery of oil, had remained much the same for centuries and the people relied on what little could be coaxed from the reluctant land. The date palms of the oases were of great importance: their fruit is highly nutritious and, when boiled, keeps for several months; their stones were crushed for fodder or made into a form of coffee; their trunks were used for building; their fibres made into baskets and bindings; and their leaf stems used for constructing 'arish houses – lightweight structures, the open-weave pattern of which permitted any passing breeze to cool the interior. Other buildings were constructed of mud brick, often around a central courtyard, an architectural style that remains in some modern domestic buildings to this day.

Early education

Since Sheikh Zayed had received only basic instruction in the principles of Islam from a local *mu'allim*, or teacher of the Holy Qur'an, it was one of his priorities that Sheikh Khalifa and his siblings receive a comprehensive education. It was vital that, from an early age, they were encouraged to recognize and prepare for the roles they would one day play in the governing of the country. To this end, Sheikh Khalifa was educated primarily in Al Ain, received further education at the Royal Military Academy at Sandhurst in the United Kingdom and, from then on, accompanied his father on innumerable occasions in Sheikh Zayed's role as Ruler's Representative. This valuable apprenticeship allowed Sheikh Khalifa to gain knowledge of the people and learn the delicate nuances and arts of leadership, wisdom, local politics and Arabic values.

Even though Sheikh Khalifa was handed the reins of power relatively late in life (at 56 years of age), he'd been the ruler-in-waiting for many years. His father began to groom him for high office at a young age so that, when the time came, there would be a seamless, consistent and stable transition from father to son. To that end, Sheikh Zayed entrusted him, along with his brothers, with more and more duties so that Sheikh Khalifa assumed responsibility for the majority of the emirate's domestic affairs before his father died.

Training began in earnest when Sheikh Zayed took over as Ruler of Abu Dhabi from his brother Sheikh Shakhbut in 1966, and the 18-year-old Sheikh Khalifa succeeded his father as Ruler's Representative in Abu Dhabi's Eastern Region on September 18, 1966. He was also appointed as Head of the Al Ain Courts Department. During his short, two-and-a-half-year tenure, Sheikh Khalifa oversaw the construction of the Hilton Hotel and the main highway between Abu Dhabi and Al Ain, and even introduced DC3 (Dakota) flights between the two towns, thus reinforcing Abu Dhabi's unequivocal ownership and stewardship of Al Ain. With such hands-on training, this intensely private man soon learned the value of consultation, decision and resolution.

Expanding portfolios

On February 1, 1969, Sheikh Khalifa was named Crown Prince of Abu Dhabi and the next day, was appointed Head of the Abu Dhabi Department of Defence. During his term, he was responsible for building up the Abu Dhabi Defence Force, which was to become the core of the fledgling UAE Armed Forces.

A few months prior to Federation, in July 1971, Sheikh Khalifa became the Head of the Council of Ministers of Abu Dhabi and Minister of Defence and Finance. And, with the birth of the United Arab Emirates on December 2, 1971, he was appointed as the new country's Deputy Prime Minister. When he was sworn in, he was equipped with impressive skills for his young age.

At the beginning of 1974, following the dissolution of Abu Dhabi's separate Council of Ministers, Sheikh Khalifa was appointed as the Chairman of the new Abu Dhabi Executive Council. The council oversaw the implementation of a comprehensive programme of development to construct houses, roads, water and electricity facilities and other fundamental elements and services required for a modern city infrastructure – all within a few years. Indeed, Sheikh Khalifa

was so committed to these development projects that he personally supervised the construction of some 16 government hospitals dotted round the emirate, as well as opening more than 370 private clinics and 12 private hospitals.

This commitment is still evident to this day. For example, in November 2005, a new diabetes centre was opened in Sheikh Khalifa Medical City (SKMC). It was staffed by eight doctors, 10 nurses, four diabetes educators, two clinical dieticians, a pharmacist, a podiatrist, translators and clerical staff, who provide state-of-the-art care for diabetes sufferers and offer enhanced services such as insulin pump therapy and a 96-hour continuous blood-glucose monitoring facility.

Following his success with the pre-Federation Abu Dhabi Department of Defence, Sheikh Khalifa was appointed to the position of Deputy Supreme Commander of the UAE's Armed Forces in May 1976. He contributed considerably to the make up and modernization of the military, and was heavily involved in the establishment of training centres and the procurement of the most sophisticated weapons technology.

Today, the UAE armed forces, based in Abu Dhabi, consist of some 65,500 personnel, 4,000 of whom belong to the UAE Air Force. Deliveries of 80 US F-16 fighter aircraft, to complement its existing arsenal of French Mirage 2000-9s, UK Hawk aircraft, transport planes, and US Apache and French Puma helicopters, began in May 2005.

The UAE Navy is made up of 2,500 personnel and, although the smallest of the country's armed forces, possesses 12 coastal patrol boats and eight missile craft.

Sheikh Khalifa has also enjoyed tenure as Chairman of the Abu Dhabi Fund for Development (ADFD) and the Abu Dhabi Investment Authority (ADIA).

As the former Chairman of the Environmental Research and Wildlife Development Agency (ERWDA), now the Environment Agency – Abu Dhabi (EAD), Sheikh Khalifa is keenly aware of the importance of environmental issues and their symbiosis within a modern, industrial conurbation. "The protection of the environment is not a sort of lavishness, but is a national duty which must be established and developed in the conscience of people," he has stated, adding that, "clean technologies that achieve harmony between economic, social and environmental elements must be implemented to protect the environment."

In 1989, Sheikh Khalifa established the National Avian Research Centre (NARC), now also part of EAD, which is committed to the sustainable use of wildlife and captive breeding programmes. This was followed in September 2005 by a new law, issued by Sheikh Khalifa, which prohibited the act of hunting mammals, birds and reptiles in Abu Dhabi without a licence from EAD.

Reaping the petrodollar rewards

Just like his father, Sheikh Khalifa took a keen interest in the oil industry and oversaw the transformation of the settlement of Abu Dhabi in his role as President of the Supreme Petroleum Council (SPC), ploughing the revenue from oil back into Abu Dhabi's infrastructure and also seeking ways to diversify the economy away from its dependence on the production of oil and gas. This included investment in petrochemicals and improving the emirate's industrial facilities with the construction of the Ruwais Industrial Area adjacent to the Jebel Dhanna Terminal in the west of the country.

He was also concerned that UAE nationals should share in and reap the rewards of the country's new wealth and, to that end, Sheikh Khalifa established the Abu Dhabi

Department of Social Services and Commercial Buildings in 1981, otherwise known as the Khalifa Committee, which provides low-interest loans to Emiratis for construction projects and alleviates the burden placed upon them by loan repayments to commercial banks.

A decade later, in 1991, he built upon these foundations by establishing the Private Loans Authority, enabling more nationals to construct the properties they required for residential and investment properties. This was followed by the liberalization of the real-estate sector for both UAE nationals and expatriates in 2005, with Sheikh Khalifa issuing a law regulating the ownership of 99-year leasehold property in certain areas of Abu Dhabi, paving the way for numerous investment opportunities in residential and commercial property throughout the emirate.

Early in the new millennium, Sheikh Zayed began to take a lesser role in the affairs of the state as his health began to deteriorate, and Sheikh Khalifa, with the support of the Al Nahyan family, effectively took over the running of the government.

Sheikh Khalifa's apprenticeship allowed him to gain knowledge of the people of the Emirate of Abu Dhabi and beyond, and learn the delicate nuances and arts of leadership, wisdom, local politics and Arabic values. He is pictured (above) with his father Sheikh Zayed, and with his younger brother, Sheikh Sultan (right) in the late 1960s.

Top left: Sheikh Khalifa signs a document in the late 1960s, while his private secretary, Zuhair Abu Aldeeb looks on.

Centre left: Sheikh Khalifa discusses a humorous point with Sheikh Zayed's secretary, Ahmed Obaid Ali.

Bottom left: Sheikh Khalifa, dressed in Western attire in his hotel room in Beirut, Lebanon, studies a special Abu Dhabi issue of Noor Ali Rashid's magazine, *Arabian Gulf Trade,* in 1968.

Opposite page, top left: Sheikh Khalifa, with Sheikh Mubarak, the Minister of the Interior, inspects a Guard of Honour at Abu Dhabi Airport.

Opposite page, top right: Sheikh Khalifa with the country's first Minister of the Interior, Sheikh Mubarak (who is also Sheikh Khalifa's cousin), and a British journalist at Abu Dhabi Airport, during the construction of the airport in the late 1960s.

Opposite page, centre left: At a meeting of the Trucial States Development Council in Dubai. The council was created in 1965 and met twice a year.

Opposite page, centre right: Sheikh Khalifa at Abu Dhabi Airport in the late 1960s, with Sheikh Mubarak and Colonel Wilson, then Commander of the Abu Dhabi Defence Force, which was established in 1965.

Opposite page, bottom left: Sheikh Khalifa and his brother, Sheikh Sultan, in 1966, when Sheikh Zayed became Ruler of Abu Dhabi.

Opposite page, bottom right: Sheikh Khalifa with Sheikh Faisal bin Sultan Al Qasimi (right) and Ahmed bin Khalifa Al Suwaidi, who was to become Foreign Minister of the UAE, at Sheikh Khalifa's palace in Abu Dhabi.

RIGHT: Even though he was handed the reins of power after a long apprenticeship, Sheikh Khalifa had in fact been the ruler-in-waiting for a number of years. His father, Sheikh Zayed, began to groom him for office from a young age so that, when the time came for him to take over, the transition would be seamless.

BOTTOM: Taking coffee with the Ruler of Dubai, Sheikh Rashid bin Saeed Al Maktoum, during a camel race to celebrate the wedding of Sheikh Rashid's first-born son, Sheikh Maktoum.

OPPOSITE PAGE: Sheikh Khalifa accompanied his father Sheikh Zayed on numerous official visits around the emirates. Here they bid farewell to dignitaries at Abu Dhabi Airport in the early 1970s.

FROM LEFT TO RIGHT: **A line-up of VIPs: Ahmed Al Suwaidi, Sheikh Khalifa, Mana Saeed Al Otaiba, Sheikh Rashid and Sheikh Zayed bid a friendly farewell to a state guest at Abu Dhabi Airport – state occasions such as these all formed part of the grooming of a president.**

Sheikh Khalifa with Sheikh Rashid's second son, Sheikh Hamdan, during one of the federation meetings held between 1968 and 1971. Sitting on Sheikh Hamdan's right is adviser Ahmed bin Sulayem. These gatherings provided valuable lessons for the young sheikhs.

TOP LEFT: Sheikh Khalifa, with the Ruler's Guards, enjoys the spectacle of a camel race during the festivities at Sheikh Maktoum bin Rashid Al Maktoum's wedding to Sheikha Alia bint Khalifa Al Maktoum in 1971. The guard on the far left is wearing a *khanjar*, a traditional dagger.

CENTRE LEFT: Sheikh Khalifa shares a light moment with Abu Alwan, an Iraqi businessman (extreme left) who settled in Dubai in the early 1960s, along with a number of other Iraqi dignitaries.

BOTTOM LEFT: With Sheikh Rashid, the Ruler of Dubai, in October 1976.

OPPOSITE PAGE, TOP LEFT AND TOP RIGHT: Two portraits of Sheikh Khalifa.

OPPOSITE PAGE, CENTRE LEFT: Sheikh Khalifa and legal adviser, Tariq Mutwali, with members of the Japanese Friendship Society in Al Ain in the 1970s.

OPPOSITE PAGE, CENTRE RIGHT: Sheikh Khalifa being interviewed by a Lebanese journalist in the 1970s.

OPPOSITE PAGE, BOTTOM LEFT: During a federation meeting in the company of a Sharjah representative, Ibrahim Al Midfa. Al Midfa was a renowned writer, and adviser to four of Sharjah's rulers. His *majlis*, now a popular destination for visitors to Sharjah's Heritage Area, contains a famous, round windtower, with distinctive, inlaid ceramic tiles.

OPPOSITE PAGE, BOTTOM RIGHT: Pictured during a federation meeting, from right to left, the Ruler of Abu Dhabi, Sheikh Zayed; Ahmed bin Khalifa Al Suwaidi, the Minister of Foreign Affairs; Sheikh Khalifa bin Zayed, Crown Prince of Abu Dhabi; and Sheikh Ahmed bin Hamed Al Hamed.

FROM LEFT TO RIGHT: Sheikh Mohammed bin Khalifa Al Nahyan, Sheikh Khalifa bin Zayed Al Nahyan and Sheikh Mubarak bin Mohammed Al Nahyan.

The former Indian President, Dr Fakhruddin Ali Ahmed, enjoying a banquet in the mid 1970s in Abu Dhabi, with Sheikh Zayed and Sheikh Khalifa.

ABOVE: Taken during military manoeuvres in Al Ain. Sheikh Mubarak and Sheikh Khalifa
entertain Sheikh Maktoum bin Rashid Al Maktoum of Dubai.

OPPOSITE PAGE, TOP LEFT AND RIGHT: On February 1, 1969, Sheikh Khalifa was named as Crown
Prince of Abu Dhabi and the next day, he was appointed as Head of the Abu Dhabi
Department of Defence. During his term of office, he was responsible for building up the Abu
Dhabi Defence Force, which was to become the core of the fledgling UAE Armed Forces.

OPPOSITE PAGE, BOTTOM: Sheikh Khalifa and Sheikh Zayed at Sheikh Zayed's Accession Day parade.

ABOVE: In the late 1980s, Sheikh Khalifa visits Sheikh Rashid bin Saeed Al Maktoum, the Ruler of Dubai, at his Za'abeel Palace in Dubai, to enquire after his health. Also present is Sheikh Mohammed bin Rashid Al Maktoum on the right.

OPPOSITE PAGE, TOP: There has always been a strong bond between Abu Dhabi's Al Nahyan and Dubai's Al Maktoum ruling families. Here, Sheikh Khalifa and Sheikh Maktoum meet at Sheikh Zayed's Khawaneej Palace in Dubai.

OPPOSITE PAGE, BOTTOM: Sheikh Mohammed bin Rashid Al Maktoum congratulates Sheikh Khalifa on the occasion of the wedding of his son, Sheikh Sultan.

ABOVE: Sheikh Khalifa greets his father, Sheikh Zayed, with great affection.

OPPOSITE PAGE, TOP: With his uncle and former Ruler of Abu Dhabi, Sheikh Shakhbut bin Sultan Al Nahyan, in 1983, six years before the latter's death.

OPPOSITE PAGE, BOTTOM: Sheikh Khalifa with Sheikh Nahyan bin Mubarak Al Nahyan in the 1990s.

Above: **A relaxed moment away from the duties of state.**

Opposite page, top left: **Sheikh Khalifa with his brother, Sheikh Hamdan bin Zayed Al Nahyan, in the 1990s. Sheikh Hamdan is the Deputy Prime Minister of the United Arab Emirates.**

Opposite page, top right: **Sheikh Khalifa sits for a formal portrait.**

Opposite page, bottom: **Sheikh Khalifa enjoys a moment with his father, Sheikh Zayed, and brother, Sheikh Hamdan, in 2003.**

Previous spread: **During Sheikh Sultan bin Khalifa's wedding. From left to right: Sheikh Sultan bin Khalifa, the groom; Sheikh Khalifa, Sheikh Zayed and Sheikh Saif bin Mohammed Al Nahyan, father of the bride.**

Departing on a foreign trip, the United Arab Emirates' new President inspects a guard of honour at Abu Dhabi International Airport.

Statesmanship

The President of Pakistan, General Pervez Musharraf, leaving Sheikh Khalifa's Palace on his official visit to Abu Dhabi in 2005.

Sheikh Khalifa became the Ruler of Abu Dhabi following the death of his father, the President, Sheikh Zayed bin Sultan Al Nahyan, on November 2, 2004. Although Sheikh Zayed's passing marked the end of an era, Sheikh Khalifa's involvement in the running of the country and Sheikh Zayed's far-reaching vision allowed for a smooth transition and, as a result, Abu Dhabi continued to flourish and evolve.

On the morning after Sheikh Zayed's death, newspapers quickly sold out as world leaders converged on the capital city to attend the funeral and pay tribute to Sheikh Zayed, and offer condolences to Sheikh Khalifa.

It was a long and difficult day, not only for the Al Nahyan family but also for the rulers of the UAE who, nevertheless, met that evening to elect a new President. They decided, unanimously, that Sheikh Khalifa should succeed his father. A statement issued by the Office of the President read: "The Supreme Council of the rulers of the United Arab Emirates met at Bateen Palace in Abu Dhabi. The meeting was chaired by His Highness Sheikh Maktoum bin Rashid Al Maktoum, Vice-President and Prime Minister of the UAE and Ruler of Dubai, and was attended by their Highnesses the Supreme Council members and rulers of the emirates. . . .

"The Supreme Council decided unanimously to elect His Highness Sheikh Khalifa bin Zayed Al Nahyan as President of the United Arab Emirates, to succeed His Highness the late Sheikh Zayed bin Sultan Al Nahyan. . . .

"The Supreme Council emphasized their keen desire to be loyal to the principles of leadership and the values of justice and right laid down by His Highness the late Sheikh Zayed bin Sultan Al Nahyan. The Supreme Council also expressed its full confidence that the people of the United Arab Emirates will continue to be guardians of the UAE Federation and of its achievements at all levels.

"The President, His Highness Sheikh Khalifa bin Zayed Al Nahyan, expressed his appreciation for the trust and confidence shown in him by his colleagues and brothers, the rulers of the emirates. He stressed that he was determined to continue to adhere to, and work in accordance with, the guidelines laid down by the founder of the UAE Federation, in cooperation and coordination with his colleagues, the members of the Supreme Council, to continue to foster the progress of the Federation and of all that will contribute to its stability and prosperity, as well as to the welfare of its people.

"The Supreme Council pledged that it would continue to follow the path laid down by His Highness the late Sheikh Zayed bin Sultan Al Nahyan. It expressed its hopes for the success of the President, His Highness Sheikh Khalifa bin Zayed Al Nahyan, and its hopes that he might enjoy the support of Almighty God in the post he has now assumed."

The prompt election of Sheikh Khalifa as President of the UAE was an expression of the trust the members of the Supreme Council had in his abilities to build on the achievements of Sheikh Zayed. This enabled Sheikh Khalifa to move into his new role with confidence, knowing that the whole of the UAE and his family fully supported him in the awesome task of taking over the reins of the nation from his father.

As already discussed, preparations for the succession had been carefully planned by Sheikh Zayed, and Sheikh Khalifa was well placed to make a substantial contribution to the continuing development of the UAE, having been intimately involved with the Government of Abu Dhabi for many years. He is also a man loved by his people and has built upon his father's desire to empower the women of the UAE. In fact, the Emirates's first female cabinet minister, Sheikha Lubna Al Qasimi, had been appointed to the key position of Minister for Economy and Planning the day before Sheikh Zayed died.

International relations

Sheikh Khalifa has played a key role on the international stage since the formation of the UAE in 1971, when he became Deputy Prime Minister. Not only is he a strong advocate of the six-member Gulf Cooperation Council (GCC) but, on regular state visits abroad – which began in August 1972 when he was invited to France on an armaments initiative – he has met with some of the most influential leaders in the world.

In 1976 he returned to France, telling the press: "It's not a secret that we are building a strong army that will be capable of maintaining our security and territorial integrity. This force will serve as a support to the greater Arab nation as it faces our common enemy. It is therefore not surprising that we have come to France to acquire modern weaponry. I'm here at the kind invitation of the Defence Minister and the visit culminated in a comprehensive agreement with France on various aspects of military cooperation, including the supply of modern armament of the UAE armed forces."

On his third visit to that country, in April 1977, Sheikh Khalifa held talks with President Valery Giscard d'Estaing, concluding a technical and military pact, followed by another visit in May 1983, this time meeting with the French Defence Minister, who informed him that France was ready to provide the UAE with the latest military technology in the areas of infantry, navy and air armaments.

In order to strengthen bilateral relations, Sheikh Khalifa visited Great Britain in 1984 and met with Prime Minister Margaret Thatcher and, three years later in 1987, he held talks with various US officials and the US Energy Secretary.

Between 1992 and 1993, Sheikh Khalifa held numerous meetings with French officials, including the Minister of State for Foreign Trade Affairs and Defence Minister Pierre Joxe, who reaffirmed France's commitment to ties with the UAE.

A defence pact was signed between the USA and the UAE in 1994. Other high points in Sheikh Khalifa's international activities include the first high-profile visit of a UAE official to the USA in May 1998, where Sheikh Khalifa visited Washington at the invitation of US President Bill Clinton. During the visit, he met President Clinton, Vice-President Al Gore and other senior officials of both the Senate and Congress in talks that included bilateral cooperation, trade, defence and peace in the Middle East.

In November 1999, Sheikh Khalifa received Prince Charles, the Prince of Wales, to discuss wide-ranging issues and, in May the following year, he met with the German Minister of State for Foreign Affairs to discuss economic cooperation and joint investment projects between the UAE and Germany.

Following the September 11, 2001 terrorist atrocities in New York, Sheikh Khalifa sent cables of condolence to US President George W Bush and Vice-President Dick Cheney and, the following month, during a visit to the UAE by General Tommy Franks, Commander of the US Central Command, Sheikh Khalifa outlined the UAE's determination to combat terrorism.

During 2002, Sheikh Khalifa held talks with several French and US officials and met with US Defence Secretary, Donald Rumsfeld in 2003, during his visit to the UAE.

In June 2003, Sheikh Khalifa visited France once more to meet with President Chirac. He also visited Great Britain where he met Her Majesty Queen Elizabeth II; Prince Charles, the Prince of Wales; Prince Andrew, the Duke of York; and former Prime Minister Tony Blair. During talks, Sheikh Khalifa and Mr Blair confirmed their commitment to expand upon their countries' historical ties.

Sheikh Khalifa's first official visit to a foreign country as President occurred a month into his new presidency in December 2004, when he visited Saudi Arabia.

ABOVE: Sheikh Khalifa bin Zayed Al Nahyan, President of the UAE, meeting with Sheikh Maktoum bin Rashid Al Maktoum, Vice-President and Prime Minister of the UAE.

RIGHT: Sheikh Mohammed bin Rashid Al Maktoum, visiting Sheikh Khalifa and the Al Nahyan family at the Abu Dhabi Presidential Palace during Eid. Sheikh Mohammed was the Crown Prince of Dubai at the time.

ABOVE: Sheikh Khalifa with the Ruler of Ajman, Sheikh Humaid bin Rashid Al Nuaimi, during his first visit to the emirate as President of the United Arab Emirates.

OPPOSITE PAGE, TOP: Sheikh Khalifa with the son of the Crown Prince of Ajman.

OPPOSITE PAGE, BOTTOM: Sheikh Khalifa at a reception in the company of the Ruler of Fujairah, Sheikh Hamad bin Mohammed Al Sharqi.

ABOVE: Sheikh Khalifa and Sheikh Mubarak entertain the Crown Prince of Bahrain, Sheikh Hamad bin Isa Al Khalifa, during military manoeuvres near Al Ain in the late 1960s.

OPPOSITE PAGE, TOP: Members of the ruling families gather during the wedding of Sheikh Mohammed bin Khalifa Al Nahyan at Al Bateen Palace. Left to right, the groom, Sheikh Mohammed bin Khalifa Al Nahyan; Sheikh Rashid bin Ahmed Al Mualla, Ruler of Umm al-Qaiwain; Sheikh Khalifa bin Zayed Al Nahyan, then Crown Prince of Abu Dhabi; Sheikh Hamad bin Mohammed Al Sharqi, Ruler of Fujairah; Sheikh Humaid bin Rashid Al Nuaimi, Ruler of Ajman; Sheikh Ammar bin Humaid Al Nuaimi, Crown Prince of Ajman; Sheikh Sultan bin Mohammed bin Sultan Al Qasimi, Crown Prince and Deputy Ruler of Sharjah; and Sheikh Sultan bin Zayed Al Nahyan, Deputy Prime Minister of the United Arab Emirates.

OPPOSITE PAGE, BOTTOM: Sheikh Khalifa congratulates Sheikha Lubna Al Qasimi after she is sworn in as the Minister of Economy in early 2006. Looking on is Sheikh Mohammed bin Rashid Al Maktoum and, in the background, new ministers, sheikhs, senior officials and dignitaries who attended the oath-taking ceremony.

RIGHT: Sheikh Khalifa greets King Hussein of Jordan during the monarch's official visit to Abu Dhabi in the 1970s. Looking on is Abu Dhabi's Chief of Protocol, Saeed Al Darmaki.

BELOW: Sheikh Khalifa meets Lebanese Prime Minister Sa'eb Salam, founder of Middle East Airlines, on the latter's official visit to Abu Dhabi.

OPPOSITE PAGE, TOP: Sheikh Khalifa shares a light moment with Sheikh Ahmed Zaki Yamani, the Saudi Oil Minister (right) and Mana Saeed Al Otaiba, the UAE Minister of Petroleum and Mineral Resources (left), during a refreshment break at an Opec meeting in Abu Dhabi in 1971.

OPPOSITE PAGE, BOTTOM: Flanked by Sheikh Khalifa, Kuwait's Oil Minister, who was also the President of the Organization of the Petroleum Exporting Companies (Opec), presides over the 1971 conference in Abu Dhabi. Opec was founded by 13 countries, including seven Arab nations, in 1960.

ABOVE: Egypt's President, Hosni Mubarak, comforts Sheikh Khalifa during the funeral of his father, the late President of the United Arab Emirates, Sheikh Zayed, in November 2004.

OPPOSITE PAGE, TOP: Sultan Qaboos bin Said of the Sultanate of Oman is received by Sheikh Zayed's son and the new President of the UAE, Sheikh Khalifa bin Zayed Al Nahyan.

OPPOSITE PAGE, BOTTOM: Syrian President Bashar Al Assad is received by Sheikh Khalifa.

ABOVE: Sheikh Khalifa deep in discussion with former French President, Jacques Chirac.

OPPOSITE PAGE, TOP: Sheikh Khalifa with US Under-Secretary of State, Richard Armitage.

OPPOSITE PAGE, BOTTOM: Crown Prince Felipe of Spain offers condolences to Sheikh Khalifa.

RIGHT: From left to right, Dr Sheikh Sultan bin Mohammed Al Qasimi, Ruler of Sharjah, Sheikh Saqr bin Mohammed Al Qasimi, the Ruler of Ra's al-Khaimah, and King Abdullah II of Jordan offer their condolences to Sheikh Khalifa at the funeral of his father, Sheikh Zayed.

BELOW: Meeting with veteran Iraqi politician, Adnan Pachachi, who lived in exile in the UAE between 1971 and 2003. Pachachi returned to Iraq in 2003 and became a member of the Iraqi Governing Council.

OPPOSITE PAGE, BOTTOM: Sheikh Khalifa and Sheikh Mohammed bin Rashid Al Maktoum entertain Qatar's former First Deputy Prime Minister and Minister of Foreign Affairs, Sheikh Hamad bin Jassim bin Jabr Al Thani, at Abu Dhabi's Wathba camel races.

The United Arab Emirates and Great Britain enjoy a cordial relationship that stretches back to 1820. As seen in the photo of Sheikh Zayed and Queen Elizabeth II above, the relationship clearly extends to the ruling families – the Nahyans and the Windsors – of the two countries.

LEFT: Sheikh Khalifa receives Queen Elizabeth II alongside the royal yacht *Britannia*, during an official visit by the British monarch to the United Arab Emirates in 1979. Also present are the the Ruler of Ajman, Sheikh Humaid bin Rashid Al Nuaimi, standing in line next to Sheikh Khalifa; and the Ruler of Umm al-Qaiwain, Sheikh Rashid bin Ahmad Al Mu'alla, standing next to Sheikh Humaid.

BELOW: Prince Andrew, the Duke of York, being welcomed by Sheikh Mansour bin Zayed Al Nahyan at his wedding banquet hosted by Sheikh Khalifa.

RIGHT: The President meeting the former Indian President, Dr APJ Abdul Kalam, on his visit to the United Arab Emirates.

BELOW: With the former Pakistani Prime Minister, Shaukat Aziz.

OPPOSITE PAGE: FIFA President Joseph S Blatter honours Crown Prince Sheikh Khalifa with a medal during the FIFA World Youth Championship, hosted by the United Arab Emirates in 2003.

ABOVE: Sheikh Khalifa and Sheikh Mohammed bin Rashid Al Maktoum meet in December 2005, shortly before Sheikh Mohammed became Vice-President of the United Arab Emirates and Ruler of Dubai following the death of his brother, Sheikh Maktoum.

OPPOSITE PAGE, TOP: Sheikh Mohammed bin Rashid Al Maktoum, left, confers with his namesake, Sheikh Mohammed bin Zayed Al Nahyan.

OPPOSITE PAGE, BOTTOM: Ruler's Representative in Abu Dhabi's Eastern Region, Sheikh Tahnoon bin Mohammed Al Nahyan, right, meets with Sheikh Mohammed bin Rashid Al Maktoum, while Sheikh Hamdan bin Zayed Al Nahyan looks on.

Sheikh Khalifa and Sheikh Mohammed bin Rashid Al Maktoum seen with the seventh UAE Cabinet formed by Sheikh Mohammed and announced on 9 February, 2006, just over a month after Sheikh Maktoum bin Rashid Al Maktoum died.

FRONT ROW FROM LEFT TO RIGHT: Mariam Mohammed Khalfan Al Roumi, Minister of Social Affairs; Sheikh Hamdan bin Mubarak Al Nahyan, Minister of Public Works; Sheikh Abdullah bin Zayed Al Nahyan, Foreign Minister; Sheikh Hamdan bin Zayed Al Nahyan, Deputy Prime Minister; Sheikh Mohammed bin Rashid Al Maktoum, Vice-President and Prime Minister and Minister of Defence of the UAE and Ruler of Dubai; Sheikh Khalifa bin Zayed Al Nahyan, President of the UAE and Ruler of Abu Dhabi; Sheikh Sultan bin Zayed Al Nahyan, Deputy Prime Minister; Sheikh Hamdan bin Rashid Al Maktoum, Minister of Finance and Industry; Lieutenant Sheikh Saif bin Zayed Al Nahyan, Minister of Interior; Sheikh Mansour bin Zayed Al Nahyan, Minister of Presidential Affairs; Sheikh Nahyan bin Mubarak Al Nahyan, Minister of Higher Education and Scientific Research; and Sheikha Lubna Al Qasimi, Minister of Economy.

BACK ROW FROM LEFT TO RIGHT: Dr Mohammed Saeed Al Kindi, Minister of Environment and Water; Dr Anwar Mohammed Gargash, Minister of State for Federal National Council Affairs; Humaid Mohammed Obaid Al Qutami, Minister of Health; Mohammed Abdullah Al Gergawi, Minister of State for Cabinet Affairs; Dr Ali bin Abdullah Al Ka'abi, Minister of Labour; Dr Mohammed Khalfan bin Kharbash, Minister of State for Financial and Industrial Affairs; Mohammed bin Nakhira Al Dhahiri, Minister of Justice; Mohammed bin Dha'en Al Hamili, Minister of Energy; Sultan bin Saeed Al Mansour, Minister of Government Sector Development; Mohammed Hussain Al Sha'ali, Minister of State for Foreign Affairs; Dr Hanif Hassan, Minister of Education; and Abdul Rahman Mohammed Al Owais, Minister of Culture, Youth and Community Development.

A modern man of tradition

Sheikh Khalifa remains in touch with his people and caters to their welfare with generosity and benevolence.

Sheikh Khalifa, while keeping one eye firmly on the future, ensures the other keeps stock of the customs of the past. Despite the phenomenal changes witnessed in his lifetime, much of the country's traditional heritage still continues to thrive today.

The values and beliefs of Islam lie at the heart of life in the United Arab Emirates, providing a source of strength and inspiration. The performance of religious duties prevails today as it has done for centuries although, in accordance with the fundamentally tolerant nature of Islam, freedom of worship is guaranteed for those of many other faiths. The dynamics of a vibrant economy are not overlooked, of course, but shorter working hours are prescribed during the fasting month of Ramadan, while festivals such as Eid al-Adha and Eid al-Fitr are public holidays for all.

Celebrations remain largely as they have for centuries and many of the songs and dances handed down from generation to generation have survived to the present. The *na'ashat*, the traditional dance during which colourfully dressed young women swirl their hair to the rhythm of the music, and the insistent Arabian music itself, are just two examples. Traditional dancing is always in evidence at major modern-day occasions such as National Day celebrations on December 2, which occur throughout the country, while the traditional dress – the *dishdasha* or *kandoura* worn by UAE national men and the *abaya* worn by UAE national women – reinforces a strong sense of cultural identity.

Many of the emirate's traditional buildings, such as Qasr al-Hosn and the ancient watchtower at Maqta'a Bridge, and a number of forts and watchtowers in Al Ain and the Liwa Crescent, have been restored. Qasr al-Hosn marked the starting point of the growth of Abu Dhabi and is still one of its most famous landmarks, although the surrounding high-rise towers dwarfing it are certainly very different from the palm-frond '*arish* dwellings over which it looked not too long ago.

The creation of heritage villages around the UAE, including in the city of Abu Dhabi itself, is another project designed to preserve the knowledge of the past. These villages, which showcase traditional arts, crafts and lifestyles of the region, including replicas of pearl-diving villages and Bedu camps, are becoming tourist attractions in their own right.

Traditional souks, too, are as much a part of any tourist itinerary as the air-conditioned shopping malls for which the UAE is justifiably famous. Indeed, the fact that so much Arabian culture and heritage remains in the UAE is a major factor in ensuring its success as a tourist destination.

The link with old and new extends to the sporting life, where the age-old pastimes of falconry, camel-racing (for which Sheikh Khalifa is well known for his patronage) and dhow racing sit comfortably alongside more modern-day pursuits such as golf, cricket, rugby, aerobatics and powerboat racing.

The philanthropist

Sheikh Khalifa, recognizing his privileged position, has for many years sought ways to provide for the community he now leads, and cater to the welfare of his people with generosity and benevolence. He remains in touch with his people by holding a series of open *majlis*, where UAE nationals can meet him to discuss their problems or worries.

In 2000, the Sheikh Khalifa Excellence Awards were introduced by the Abu Dhabi Chamber of Commerce and Industry (ADCCI) to recognize organizational achievement in terms of quality and performance. This was followed by the Sheikh Khalifa Industrial Awards. These awards have since been merged into one collection of quality awards to focus corporate endeavours, increase productivity and enhance the awards' reputation and status, and have been recognized by the European Foundation of Quality Management (EFQM) and the British Quality Foundation.

Sheikh Khalifa is a great believer in the power of education, not just at home, but abroad too, and he has supported numerous educational institutions, including the University of Wales, Lampeter (the third oldest university in Wales and England after Cambridge and Oxford) where he funded the construction of the new purpose-built Sheikh Khalifa Building, inaugurated in 1997, which houses the university's Department of Theology, Religious and Islamic Studies.

His philanthropy extends to several Islamic causes as he endeavours to ease the suffering of his less-fortunate Arab brothers around the region. He is involved with numerous humanitarian projects and construction initiatives, such as the establishment of an entire city bearing his name – Khalifa City – in the Gaza Strip in collaboration with the United Nations Relief Work Agency (UNRWA) and the Palestine National Authority, which will home Palestinians in areas formerly occupied by Israel. Expected to house some 30,000 to 40,000 people, and costing some US$100 million, the foundation stone was laid in October 2005 by Sheikh Khalifa's brother, Sheikh Abdullah bin Zayed Al Nahyan, then the Minister of Information and Culture, in the presence of Palestinian President, Mahmoud Abbas.

As Chairman of the Abu Dhabi Fund for Development (ADFD), Sheikh Khalifa's role is to oversee the country's programme of overseas aid and, as such, the UAE was one of the first to respond to the aftermath of Hurricane Katrina, despatching emergency relief supplies, including medicines, medical equipment, food, tents and clothing to the victims of the hurricane, which devastated several US states in the last quarter of 2005.

And an agreement was signed in October 2005 to build Sheikh Khalifa City in Banda Aceh, the district in Indonesia devastated by the December 2004 tsunami. The US$5.07 million project between the UAE Government, the Red Crescent Authority, the United Nations Development Programme, UN-Habitat and the Indonesian Government, is set to house more than 1,000 families.

A bright tomorrow

Sheikh Khalifa's forward-thinking approach continues to make its mark, not just in the Emirate of Abu Dhabi, but throughout the country as a whole. He has ushered in a new era; a modern, groundbreaking, 21st-century era. There's little doubt that Sheikh Khalifa will continue to drive the United Arab Emirates towards even greater successes than those witnessed under Sheikh Zayed's dynamic stewardship, and build upon his stable and secure legacy towards a bright tomorrow.

ABOVE: Training young falconers in Al Bateen Palace with Sheikh Mohammed, the son of Sheikh Nahyan bin Mubarak Al Nahyan sitting in the centre. The traditional sport of falconry remains very popular in the United Arab Emirates and falcons command very high prices.

OPPOSITE PAGE: Falcons require intense training and conditioning to reach peak performance.

ABOVE: Arabs have remained keen falconers and the sport preserves their ties to the desert.

OPPOSITE PAGE: The spectacular traditional dance – the *na'ashat* – performed by colourfully dressed girls, who swirl their hair to the insistent rhythm of the accompanying music, takes place during a wedding in Abu Dhabi.

FOLLOWING SPREAD: Folk dancing is also enjoyed by Emarati men of all ages.

ABOVE: Camels are an important part of the UAE heritage and camel racing is a popular sport.

PREVIOUS SPREAD: Everyone joins in the dance on festive occasions – on this occasion Abdul Jalil Al Fahim and Sheikh Saif bin Mohammed Al Nahyan lead the proceedings.

Western reef herons, accompanied by a migrant great egret and a solitary crow, surround
the United Arab Emirates flag on a traditional dhow.

Family first

ABOVE: Sheikh Khalifa with his first-born son, Sheikh Sultan.

OPPOSITE PAGE: Sheikh Khalifa attending an Abu Dhabi school function with his father in the mid 1960s.

Family lies at the heart of Arab traditions and nowhere is this more amply demonstrated than by Sheikh Khalifa's commitment to the elderly of the nation, with health institutions, ministries and public utilities among other establishments providing for and ensuring psychological harmony for UAE nationals in their twilight years.

In keeping with tradition, due respect is accorded to elder members and bonds are strong within extended families. In this regard, Sheikh Khalifa is no exception and, as head of the ruling family – and despite his many responsibilities – he maintains close contact with his kin. He enjoys the more informal get-togethers and the occasion of family weddings, or sporting occasions, which provide time for relaxation. Although he believes strongly in the value of work, in his spare time he enjoys the sport of falconry, fishing, poetry and reading.

Sheikh Khalifa has several children with his wife, Sheikha Shamsa (a member of the Mazrui tribe, part of the Bani Yas confederation), including Dr Sheikh Sultan bin Khalifa and Sheikh Mohammed bin Khalifa, along with numerous grandchildren such as Sheikh Zayed bin Sultan and Sheikh Mohammed bin Sultan.

Dr Sheikh Sultan bin Khalifa bin Zayed Al Nahyan was born in 1965 in Al Ain. He is a member of the Abu Dhabi Executive Council, Chief of the Abu Dhabi Crown Prince's Court and Chairman of the UAE Equestrian and Racing Federation (UAEERF).

He obtained a Bachelor's degree in political and administrative sciences from the Emirates University in 1985, after which he attended the Zayed bin Sultan Military College in Al Ain, graduating in 1988.

He built upon these excellent military foundations by attending the Royal Military Academy, Sandhurst, in the UK, where he graduated in 1989. After the graduation he obtained a Master's degree in Political Science from the University of Salford, Manchester, UK.

In November 1996, he was awarded the Rashid Prize for Academic Excellence for his dissertation 'The Geopolitics of the United Arab Emirates' and, two years later, in November 1998, he received a Doctorate (PhD) in International Studies from the University of Limerick, Ireland. Another Doctorate followed from Nasser Higher Military Academy in Egypt in April 1999 for his dissertation, 'The National Security of the UAE in the Light of Regional and Global Changes'.

Dr Sheikh Sultan bin Khalifa achieved Lieutenant Colonel Staff (PSC) pilot status in 1999 and, in 2000, he obtained the rank of Colonel Staff (PSC). He has enjoyed tenure in other roles, including Honorary Chairman of Abu Dhabi Chamber of Commerce and Industry, Honorary Chairman of the International Union for Maritime Sport for Asia and the Middle East, and Chairman of the Abu Dhabi International Club for Maritime Sport. He is a keen sportsman, enjoys falconry and breeds Arabian horses.

In March 2004, Dr Sheikh Sultan was awarded honorary membership to the International College of Surgeons by World President-Elect of the International College of Surgeons, Professor Nadey Hakim.

Sheikh Mohammed bin Khalifa bin Zayed Al Nahyan, Sheikh Khalifa's second and youngest son, was born in the

early 1980s. He enjoys traditional dhow-sailing races and owns several racing craft. He has undertaken various roles in the government, including within the Pensions Department, which was followed by a move into the prestigious role of Chairman of the Abu Dhabi Finance Department. He is also a member of the Supreme Petroleum Council (SPC). Complementing his father's commitment to education, Sheikh Mohammed has also enjoyed tenure as Chairman of the Awards' Council of Trustees for the Sheikh Khalifa bin Zayed Award for Teachers, which venerates educational excellence and those who contribute to the promotion of education and educational standards throughout the country.

ABOVE: A rare formal photograph of Sheikh Zayed with all his sons.

OPPOSITE PAGE: Father and son. A charming photograph of Sheikh Khalifa, when he was Crown Prince of Abu Dhabi, with his son Sheikh Sultan, then Chairman of the Crown Prince's Court.

ABOVE: A childhood group portrait taken in 1960s: Sheikh Sultan bin Zayed, with his brothers Mohammed, Hamdan and Hazza and their caretaker at a garden in Al Ain.

BELOW RIGHT: Seen from right to left, Sheikh Mohammed bin Zayed, Sheikh Hamdan bin Zayed and Sheikh Hazza bin Zayed with their sister.

OPPOSITE PAGE: Rare portraits of four of Sheikh Khalifa's brothers as young boys: Sheikh Mohammed bin Zayed, top left; Sheikh Hamdan bin Zayed, top right; Sheikh Hazza bin Zayed, bottom left; and Sheikh Sultan bin Zayed, bottom right.

ABOVE: Sheikh Zayed, accompanied by his son, Sheikh Mohammed, and companions on a bird shoot during a private visit to England.

OPPOSITE PAGE, TOP: Some Al Nahyan brothers during a London visit with their father Sheikh Zayed.

OPPOSITE PAGE, BOTTOM: Sheikh Zayed on holiday in Lausanne, Switzerland, with his sons, Sheikh Hamdan bin Zayed and Sheikh Hazza bin Zayed.

ABOVE LEFT: The late Sheikh Shakhbut bin Sultan Al Nahyan, Sheikh Khalifa's uncle and former Ruler of Abu Dhabi, during a Trucial States Council meeting in Dubai in the early 1960s.

ABOVE RIGHT: A prominent member of the Al Nahyan family, Sheikh Mohammed bin Khalifa Al Nahyan, grandson of Sheikh Zayed bin Khalifa and father of Sheikhs Hamdan, Mubarak, Tahnoun, Saif, Surour and Saeed, was for many years the highly-respected elder of the family. He died in 1979.

OPPOSITE PAGE, TOP: Entering Qasr al-Hosn, Sheikh Zayed is accompanied by Crown Prince Sheikh Khalifa, right, and Sheikh Hamdan bin Mohammed, left, during his first years of rule. Qasr al-Hosn is, today, a museum and a part of the Abu Dhabi Cultural Foundation.

OPPOSITE PAGE, BOTTOM: Sheikh Zayed and Sheikh Khalifa, along with the rulers of the other emirates, attending a wedding.

ABOVE: Sheikh Mohammed bin Zayed Al Nahyan with his sons, from left to right, Sheikh Hamdan, Sheikh Khalid and Sheikh Dhiyab.

OPPOSITE PAGE, TOP: Four of the Al Nahyan brothers on the occasion of a family wedding. From left to right: Sheikh Saif, Sheikh Mohammed, Sheikh Hazza and Sheikh Saeed.

OPPOSITE PAGE, BOTTOM: Sheikh Mohammed and Sheikh Mansour participate in traditional dancing to celebrate the wedding of their brother, Sheikh Tahnoon bin Zayed Al Nahyan.

ABOVE: Wishing Sheikh Khalifa farewell on his departure for a foreign tour are Sheikh Mohammed bin Zayed, Sheikh Tahnoun bin Mohammed and Sheikh Nahyan bin Mubarak.

OPPOSITE PAGE: Sheikh Mubarak bin Mohammed Al Nahyan, centre, the former Minister of Interior, with his sons Sheikh Nahyan bin Mubarak, right, and Sheikh Hamdan bin Mubarak, left, at Al Bateen Palace in early 2000.

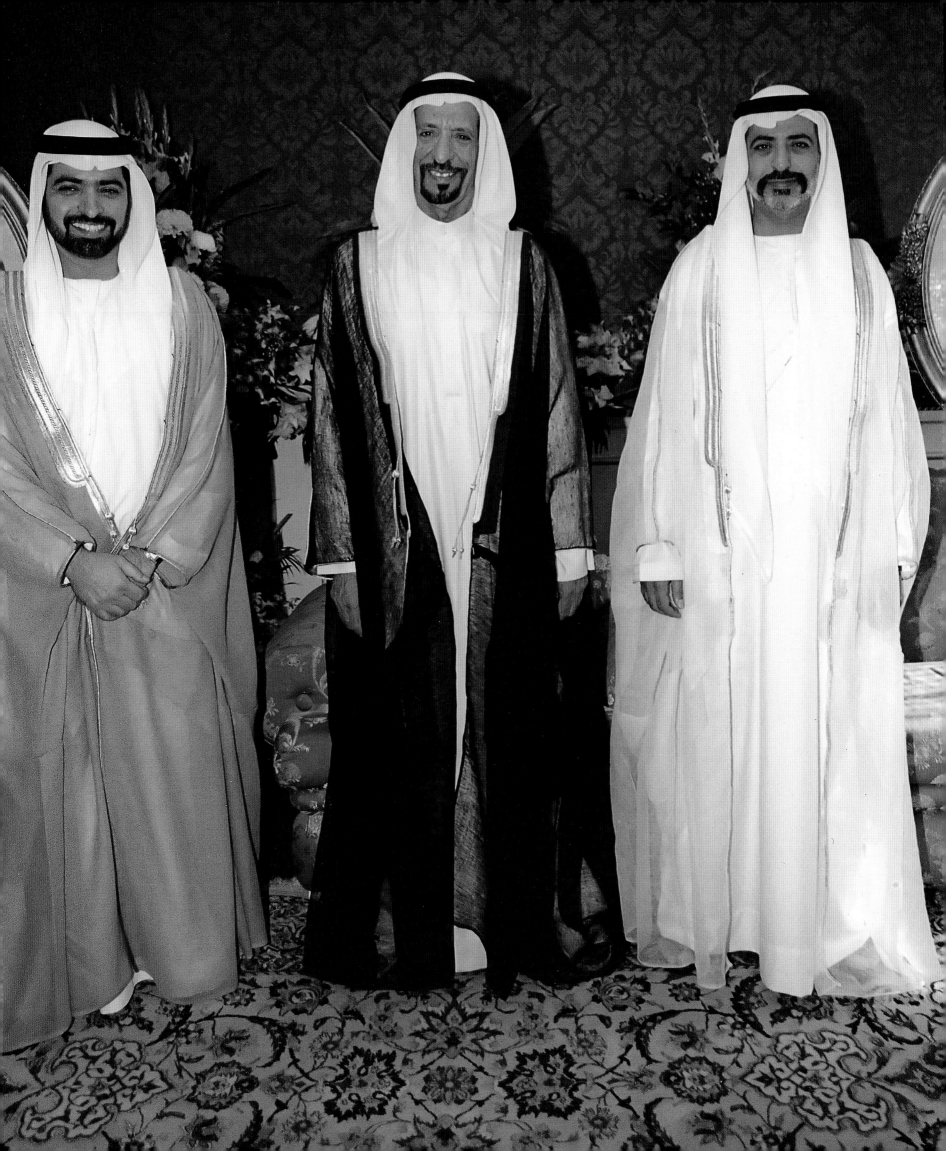

Sheikh Khalifa and his brother Sheikh Sultan discuss an important topic.

ABOVE: Sheikh Khalifa having a word with his son, Dr Sheikh Sultan, during the wedding of his younger son Sheikh Mohammed bin Khalifa.

FOLLOWING SPREAD: Sheikh Khalifa, second from left, with his brothers and family members, left to right, front row: Sheikh Sultan bin Zayed, Sheikh Khalifa bin Zayed, Sheikh Mohammed bin Zayed, Sheikh Tahnoun bin Mohammed Al Nahyan, Sheikh Mansour bin Zayed, Dr Sheikh Sultan bin Khalifa and Sheikh Sultan bin Hamdan.

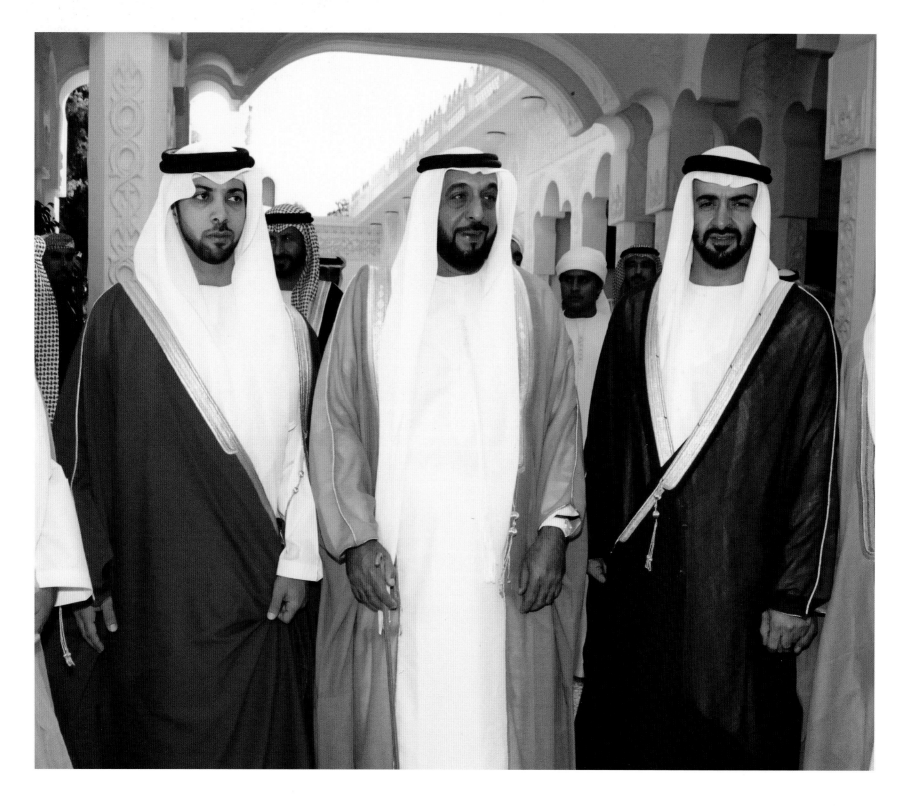

Sheikh Khalifa with his brothers, Sheikh Mohammed, right, and Sheikh Mansour.